THE DANCE OF AFRICA

THE DANCE OF AFRICA

AN INTRODUCTION

BY LEE WARREN

WITH DANCE INSTRUCTIONS ILLUSTRATED
BY HARIS PETIE
PHOTOGRAPHS BY VYVIAN D'ESTIENNE
AND OTHERS

PRENTICE-HALL, INC., ENGLEWOOD CLIFFS, N.Y.

For My Hus'
    To Whoı   793.346   ranger
                W253d
We would like ı   Sue and Elliott
Roberts for their   *ᴜ.³*   ᴢ preparation of
this book.

Printed in the United States of America • 2

Prentice-Hall International, Inc., London
Prentice-Hall of Australia, Pty. Ltd., North Sydney
Prentice-Hall of Canada, Ltd., Toronto
Prentice-Hall of India Private Ltd., New Delhi
Prentice-Hall of Japan, Inc., Tokyo

10 9 8 7 6 5 4 3

FOREWORD

Among the exciting sights and sounds of Black Africa is not only the dancing but the way it is performed. Woven throughout the pattern of African life, dancing for Africans is more than the recreation it is for Westerners. With the music which is inseparable from it, dancing is part of the process of living itself. The response of the body to expressions of love, joy, grief and despair—all to the accompaniment of music, songs, and drumming—is the heritage of the African. To see an African dance is to witness his cultural past and present. Africans use their bodies to reflect their emotions, their hopes and their religion: The head moves in one rhythm, the shoulders in another, the arms in still a third, the feet in still another. Their dance is text in motion, linked to the music of the drums, instruments and voices.

If a people's culture is its mirror, we must turn to Africa's arts in order to know Africa's peoples. And to study Africa and neglect its dance is like studying Greece without its architecture.

For the African, the fullest expression of art is dance.

CONTENTS

THE PLACE OF DANCE IN TRADITIONAL AFRICAN LIFE

Man is all. If you call "Earth," it does not respond. If you call "Clothes" or "Gold," they do not respond. Man is all.

African saying

There is no easy formula for defining traditional African dance, just as there is no thumbnail profile of the African. The only common denominator for the people south of the Sahara is a dark skin. Customs, language and behavior cover a span as wide as the great desert that cuts a swath between North and Black Africa.

It is difficult for Americans to understand that Africans are very different from each other. I can still remember my shock when a woman who heard that I was traveling to Africa asked, "Do you speak African?" as if Africa were a single country with one language, one people, one history! I think of that ingenuous lady as I wonder how to distill the essence of many countries and cultures on the African continent in one easy-to-digest capsule.

1

Africans are many different peoples, except that for all Africans, dance is an integral part of life. As modern Africa begins to adapt to the homogenizing influences of technology, she is also becoming increasingly aware of her unique and complex cultural heritage. In this heritage is a legacy of expression in dance for every member of traditional society in many aspects of living, from the time he is born until he departs to his final home in the spirit world.

For the Ibos of Nigeria, for instance, no distinction is made between professional and amateur dancers—everyone dances whether he is an accomplished dancer or not. In fact, dancing is one activity in which everyone tries to excel, because on certain occasions in one's lifetime, one just has to dance. Yet not even the most accomplished dancer ever dreamed of turning professional in the context of the traditional community, for that would subject him to as much ridicule as if he had confessed that he couldn't dance at all.

Dance is intermeshed in every aspect of day-to-day traditional African life. There are some occasions when dance is optional, but on most occasions it is mandatory. Each dance has its own music, movements, and costumes, and most fundamental of all, each dance has a function and a motivation that is understood by all members of that society. Each community has its dances for a particular use at a specific time, for a special event.

Something of this comforting familiarity is understood in the happy recognition of songs heard and sung in one's youth. Mature men and women are delighted to hear and sing "the old-time favorites." If a person grew up with "I'm Dreaming of a White Christmas," hearing that song again will bring an instantaneous response, often the urge to sing along. That is the key to understanding the relationship of traditional African dance and audience—the responsive action of singing along, joining in, being part of, being *more* than a spectator! "I'm Dreaming of a White Christmas" may never have served any more basic function than the binding of friends together in a social gathering, but the act of singing a familiar song *together* is a *communal* one. If the singing of that particular song had been absolutely essential to some phase of daily routine, one could begin to have a faint glimmer of appreciation of how vital the coalition of music and dance is in traditional African life.

A sense of community is more basic in African culture than it is in our own. Each member of a society understands his role as one unit that is part of a whole. This commitment to a mutually shared loyalty, this awareness of who one is, can be envied by Americans bedevilled with an identity crisis. The torment of isolation is uncommon in traditional African communities.

A comment that reveals the certainty of a person's place was once made to Hilda Kuper, the anthropologist, by a Swazi woman. Miss Kuper asked her if she ever danced alone. The woman answered, "One always dances alone, but stands with others." Then when she was asked if she ever danced simply for the enjoyment of it, for example, when she was alone in her hut, the woman answered, "Dance when I am alone in my hut? Am I a wizard? If I wanted to dance and I was alone, I would stand outside so that people could see me."

In the same way an African does not usually sing *for* someone but rather *with* him, his involvement with dance is totally interrelated with his people. The exception, as noted by the Swazi woman, is the wizard or priest who *does* dance alone.

A commonly held but often mistaken idea is that the *Possession* dance is designed to send the dancer *into* a trance, during which he becomes possessed by a spirit. The very opposite is usually true: The wizard dances to *rid himself* of the spirit that has become instilled in him, not to be possessed by it. Early in the morning on a day of worship, priests, elders and other officials of the community accompany the one priest who has become aware of "something special" inside him. When the spirit resides in him, the priest acts as a medium between the living, who are in need of help, and the dead, whose wisdom and guidance are transmitted through the spirit in him. It is almost as if the priest is conducting a clinic, acting as a healer for those who come to him with problems.

When the day is done and it is time for the spirit to be driven away, the drumming begins. The priest dances, whirls and propels himself in a blurred frenzy in an effort to oust the spirit within him. He dances until he finally collapses in exhaustion. Then he is taken away to a recovery area, a sort of patio, where he can sleep until the next morning.

The *Possession* dance is an exception, though, and most African dances require a measure of participation for all the members of a group. More typical is the *Ekpo* ritual performed in Nigeria, which is designed to keep the town where it is performed clean, in a state of ritual purity. It also serves to ensure the good health of the people of the town.

"We scrutinize a society to understand its art," according to Jacques Lipschitz, the sculptor, "while we examine its art to understand the society." This dual approach applies to African dance, for dance is intermeshed in many aspects of life: whatever the style and flow of movement, whatever the tempo characteristic of a particular movement, dance serves as a mirror for African life, and at the same time, as a support in the framework of its culture.

THE TRADITIONAL AFRICAN RITUAL DANCE

*You say you will dance till daybreak, but
did you ask the drummer?*

African saying

It is unrealistic to attempt to make neat groupings of the different kinds of African dance, but broadly speaking there are two basic types. Recreational dance is informal, allows for free improvisation, and closely follows the trends of popular fashion in music, ideas and standards of acceptable behavior. Ritual dance, on the other hand, is relatively unchanging, the bone and blood of African culture with deep psychological and religious roots.

Used in the context of traditional African life, the word ritual has a great many related meanings. It is primarily the act of commemorating a specific event, such as the initiation into manhood or the welcoming of the new year. The act of commemoration comes to be identified with the event and eventually becomes inseparable from it.

As timeless statements about the meaning of life, African rituals are concerned with the origins of the world, with

6

planting and harvesting, hunting, or the honoring of a king. Rituals are acts of faith in the renewal of life; they trace the order of the universe. Most of the traditional ritual dances cannot be traced with accuracy to their origins and though ritual is not *designed* as art, it is a *source* of art, of masks, music and dance. It is an art in which everyone participates, in which everyone is involved.

Ritual plays an important part in the life of any people. There is ritual in the opening of our baseball season, when a VIP throws out the first ball onto the playing field. The call "Play ball!" resounds and the game begins. This ceremony is as unchanging as our singing of "Auld Lang Syne" on New Year's Eve or the march to "Pomp and Circumstance" at graduation.

The ritual dances of traditional African society have a dimension that is missing in American ritual. Telling a story of an event in words, which is the myth, and using bodily movement to further describe and embellish it are both essential elements of the African ritual. These two, the myth and the dance, are component parts of the history of a people—truths of their way of life that are constantly being renewed.

For instance, there is the *Abofoo* dance of the Krachi people which is concerned with the preservation of physical life. It is a hunting dance, performed both before and after the hunt. First it affirms the hunter's luck necessary for a successful hunt. After the kill, *Abofoo* purifies the hunter of that special power that had been given him for the specific purpose of enabling him to achieve his victory. He *must* be rid of it once it has served his purpose.

Accompanied by drums, gongs, and both male and female singers, *Abofoo* begins with the quick movements of the Ofufuri—the cats—the leopard, the lion and the

7

panther. Swirling billowing capes worn by the dancers enhance the dancer's catlike movements, in contrast to the slow and deliberate movements that the dancer representing Konte, the elephant, makes. The elephant's dance is unique in that he stands very nearly motionless to emphasize his enormous size and strength. Occasionally the elephant dancer's left arm, which represents the trunk, lazily slaps his back.

After the dancer representing the hunter kills the animals, his trophies are collected in the ritual dance area. From the cats, the trophies are the skin and skull. From the elephant, the tusks, tail and trunk are taken. The tail, the lower jaw and the horns are taken from the buffalo. A celebration in honor of the dead animals follows, where drink is served and a libation is poured on the trophies to honor the dead animals.

As a man must hunt, a man must hoe his land. With his feet wide apart, his knees relaxed, the farmer bends down, brings the hoe to the ground, pulls it up, and moves ahead. Down to the ground, pull up from the ground, move ahead. The rhythmic regularity of the movement, the full employment of the body in an activity of production, becomes a dance.

Agriculture has spawned many ritual dances, among which is the dance of the *Tyi Wara*, an ancient homage to farming performed by the Bambara people of Mali. The Bambara believe that they were put into contact with all of the elements of the universe through agriculture. For them, farming is glorified; they believe it is man's highest accomplishment, the occupation which brings man into intimate concert with the sun, the stars, the moon, the land, and the seasons of the year.

According to the legend that the old men tell, Tyi Wara was the child of the African Eve (who is called Mousso Koroni) and a snake. Half-man, half-animal, Tyi Wara had supernatural powers potent enough to teach the Bambara of long ago how to coax grain from their poor land. Under his guidance, men could change weeds into corn.

Originally, the main purpose of the *Tyi Wara* dance was to invoke the blessing of Tyi Wara on the daily contest between the Bambara and the stubborn soil. At that time, the fields themselves were the setting for the dance. The men tilled the soil, the dancers moved next to them, and the women sang the song of the *Tyi Wara*. They sang that the men should become excellent farmers and deserve great prestige and glory, and they praised the accomplishments of their ancestors working the land, and they sang of their total commitment to the earth, the mother of us all.

Over the years, the dance gradually changed from a purely religious ritual to a more social form of entertainment. It was moved from the fields to the village square. Now dance competitions are held with the dancers participating in the hoeing contests which are called N'gala Tyi. The winners are called Tyi-n-gana, or farming champion.

The need for food runs through the folklore of every people. Not surprisingly, it is the center of many ritual and festival dances of traditional African life. Americans say, "One man's meat is another man's poison," while Nigerians say, "You have curious things to eat; I am fed on proper meat." For not only does the consumption of food relate to the health and life of a people, but the importance of the actual process of producing the food must also be acknowledged.

In America, advertising men use this principle in selling their products. They know that participation is necessary for the consumer to feel first the sense of achievement in preparing the food, and then the enjoyment of eating it. A famous success story born of this knowledge deals with the instructions on a box of cake mix.

"Add a fresh egg yourself" was the simple instruction on the box. Actually, the manufacturer would have had no problem in developing a mix that would bake up into a delicious cake *without* the addition of the egg. But he knew that adding a fresh egg was a nostalgic reminder for his customers of a time when cakes were made by measuring and mixing the basic ingredients at home. The cake mix to which one adds a fresh egg is a nonstop best seller.

In a more direct way, the link between food and its production is part of an African wisdom deeply rooted in its past and reflected in the rituals and ceremonies that persist into the present. One example is the feast of the new yam, an occasion for giving thanks to the earth goddess and to honor the ancestral spirits of the clan. It begins the season of plenty, the harvesting of the crops, and it is an occasion of joy. *Kundum*, a harvest festival dance of the Ashanti people of Ghana, is not only symbolic of rebirth and an expression of thankfulness for the fruits of the earth, but is also a time of remembering departed friends and relatives.

Another and opposite kind of commemoration of man's achievements in reaping the harvest is the *Homowo* festival of the Ga people of Ghana. *Homowo*, which means literally "hooting at hunger" is analogous to the Jewish Feast of Passover. (It is traditionally believed that the Ga people were Jews who emigrated from Egypt and settled on the land they now occupy.) Between the Nmaadum, the sowing of the wheat, and Nmaa Faa, the rite of transplanting, there is a month of silence. A strict ban is imposed on drumming, dancing and any form of merry-making that might cause noise in the town. At the end of this period, which is called Koninfemo, a lusty beating of the drums proclaims the end of the ban and the opening of the festival of the yam, the king of crops. This total absence of drumming and dance is an eloquent and intense declaration of man's dependence on the success of his crops, and a fascinating reversal of the more familiar African tradition of commemorating this happy occasion with dancing and drumming.

Over and over again, the theme of man's kinship with the soil is found in African ritual dance. "Elders of the town I greet you. If the palm tree is not well rooted in the soil, it will not bear fruit," are the words of the Ekpo praise song in which the elders of the village are compared to the earth on which the community, like a tree, relies for support and stability.

With this metaphor from agriculture, the Nigerian ritual purification is designed to keep the town clean, in a state of ritual purity, and to emphasize the importance of good health for its people. As with many African ritual dances, the *Ekpo* ritual lasts for several days during which time the dancers must visit every house to accept gifts of kola nuts and coins in exchange for their prayers.

Unlike the *Tyi Wara*, the *Ekpo* ritual not only permits but demands the involvement of women dancers as well as men. On the last day of the ritual, the women become the most important and active participants as representatives of the symbolic continuity of life in their roles as wives and mothers.

The motif of animals is central to the *Incwala*—a ritual dance of Swaziland which represents the basic dilemma of kingship. A king must be strong to lead his people, but he must also be compassionate and able to accept imperfect behavior. Men and women dressed in animal skins and feathers dance all day long. Cattle, the most valued possession of the Swazi people, must be present all during the ritual. The king, known as the lion (Ngwenyama) who shares his power with his mother, an elephant (Ndlovukati), is praised as the lion, the bull and the great mountain. Water that had been collected from all over the country, and plants from the forest are offered by special dignitaries.

In these ceremonies of hunting, farming and ritual purification, religion serves to bind men and their activity to the powers that control life. In the traditional African ritual dance, the bond between the people of the community and the supernatural powers that control them is of limitless strength. This unity gives meaning, a sense of purpose, and a sense of order to traditional African life. In the ritual dance, man is united with the cosmos, with all the elements of the universe.

Onia, a priest, dancing to an animal dance.

Children and adults make up the Coast Line troupe
which performs the dances of southern Ghana.

Kenyan girls show characteristic
movement of the Baganda dance.

The men and women who make up the Ghana Dance Ensemble, a national troupe, perform the traditional *Atsiabegkor* in costume.

THE DUAL ROLE OF TRADITIONAL AFRICAN DANCE

When a child has learned to wash his hands before meals, he is allowed to eat with his elders.

African saying

When a master hunter dies, the Hunters' Guild in Ghana holds a colorful funeral. At one funeral for a hunter who had killed 99 elephants in his lifetime, the dances performed by the dead man's fellow hunters not only paid tribute to the great hunter who had died, but also told of their own hunting skills and victories. It is the traditional African way: The ritual serves the needs of the living as much as it honors the dead.

In African funerals, the music and dance tell a sort of biography of the person who has died. His occupation, his successes, his social position in life, and the nature of his death are reflected in the funeral music and dance. And because the needs of the living are recognized as

17

being important too, the musicians will often encourage the dead man's relatives and friends to get up and *dance* to help them through the first awful agony of grief.

Funerals for members of occupational organizations— warriors and hunters, for instance—are rich in dramatic expression. In the case of the great elephant hunter, for instance, the marvel of his hunting success was mimed by dancers carrying weapons. One dancer, portraying an elephant, kept his hands stretched out in front of him to represent tusks, and moved very slowly to emphasize the elephant's huge size, very much like the elephant dancer in the *Abofoo* dance.

When a hunter dies, his son, who is supposed to inherit his father's hunting skill may dance to tell the tale of his father's prowess: "This is my father. He was a great hunter. Did he not kill this one? Did he not kill that one?"

Even more important at a funeral than the recognition of a man's accomplishments during his lifetime is the expression of group solidarity and the confirmation of a continuous loyalty to the community. The funeral of a chief, for instance, is the opportunity for all the people of the clan to acknowledge both *his* greatness and *their* enduring strength. The dance performed at a chief's funeral, therefore, serves several purposes: First, it is a public show of last respect as well as a consolation to the community; second, it creates an aura of majestic splendor that is associated with the office of a chief as well as confirming the people's sense of deep loss. The result is the further unification of the community.

When the chief is alive, he is the model of a fearless warrior; as a leader of his people he is both a kindly father and a demanding disciplinarian (remember the *Incwala* ritual representing the king's double role.) At the death of a chief, a courtier reenacts the legend of the chief by taking his place for the ceremony. As the chief is carried to the royal burial ground, the same praise songs and dances which were performed for him when he was alive are directed to the coffin. As the coffin passes from the palace to the burial place, the songs and dances are no more somber and sad than when he was alive to enjoy it. You can see how the African funeral quite neatly straddles the physical and the spirit world. Just so, when a priest dies, farewell to him may be first drummed in a sad and slow pattern, while the priestesses dance the sorrowful *Husago* dance. Then, one of the basic themes in African philosophy is stated in dance, that life always continues, if not in the living world, then in the world of the spirit. Strong and gay patterns of movement are danced to express the faith that the physically dead priest is a link between the two worlds.

In the funeral dances of the hunter, the chief and the priest, we see that there is no music and dance used solely for a funeral. What pleased a man most during his life, and which is most representative of his personality and accomplishments, is the music and dance that is appropriate for his funeral. Many African dances adapt similarly to more than one occasion. Ceremony, celebration and veneration are all woven together in dance as they are in life. The funeral dances express the importance of the community in traditional African life, in which people are bound by a shared respect for their heritage and a pride in the accomplishments of their fellow members.

This is true of many dances in various aspects of African life. For instance, an agricultural festival dance of the Irigwe people of Nigeria is performed at funerals and important state occasions as well; the *Incwala* dance is performed at the king's first marriage and at the chief's burial; in Ghana and Dahomey, the *Taki* dance is performed on three very different occasions: on Mohammed's birthday, at the installation of a chief, and for the pleasure of state visitors. The *Akan* fertility dance from Ghana is danced not only at a puberty rite but also to express joy at being alive and gratitude for the gift of life. Traditional ritual dances also serve the function of translating a personal experience into one which the community can share. The Lobi people of Ghana express their love for communal labor in the *Bobina* dance when a house is built, and *Fontomfrom*, the Ashanti military dance of the chief reenacts past military glories to inspire the people to a communal pride in his achievement.

Within the traditional community, the audience is part of a given dance because it is familiar with the social and historical background for the dance and knows what to expect. However, the audience is also *entertained* by the experience of viewing something satisfying to the eye as well as the heart. In a somewhat lesser fashion, the imaginative choreography of an American traffic policeman, used in the performance of his job, is also a source of delight to the pedestrian passersby.

African dances cannot be "only entertainment" since their roots are thrust so deeply into the African past. Whatever the experiences, beliefs and attitudes of a people are, they will be found in the movements of the dance. Every dance has a heritage which reflects the ideas of its time. Each society, each group of people, develops its own set of rules by which the structures of the dance are defined. These rules must be strictly adhered to.

"Growing up" in traditional African society is a daily learning process of both correct social behavior and correct dance behavior. Awareness of one's special place in the community begins with the knowledge that one has his father's spirit and his mother's blood. Over these formative years, the beliefs and sanctions that are the foundation for the society are repeated daily. One learns what should be done and what should not be done. So an African child comes to understand his place in the society and to master the duties attached to it. For example, only the chief, as the political and military head of the community, is entitled to dance with the sword in *Fontomfrom*.

The education of a child in traditional African life includes knowing the difference between the dances of one's people, what is permitted and what is required, what is acceptable and what is forbidden. A man would not perform the effeminate movements of the public puberty rite nor would a woman attempt the vigorous twirling and twisting of the priest performing *Ntwaaho*, the part of the *Akom* festish dances in which the priest whirls round and round as he illustrates the perfection and oneness of God. The graceful *Adowa* dance of the Ashanti people invites *everyone* to participate, but first one must learn the gestures, the symbols, the dance forms and drum patterns.

The African's knowledge of his identity is strengthened by the ancient traditions which dictate his place in society and his responsibilities. As the old saying goes, when a child has learned how to wash his hands, he can then eat with his elders.

THE MOVEMENTS OF TRADITIONAL AFRICAN DANCE

If the dance is pleasing, even the lame
will crawl to it.

African saying

For the American who is accustomed to taking his car wherever he goes, and to whom adding an egg to a cake mix is a novelty, the importance of physical exertion and expression as the traditional African life-style is difficult to understand. It was even more difficult for the European missionaries and colonists who came to Africa in the nineteenth century to understand, and they tried to suppress the traditional music and dance in an effort to curb pagan immorality. Yet try as they might, that total relationship of the body, mind and spirit that is so uniquely African did survive, and continues to flourish, defining that which is right and natural in the African's journey from childhood to old age.

Dance in Africa is part of the life-style, not something added to it. The importance of physical exertion in traditional African society, simply for survival, makes physical expression a natural outgrowth of experience. As an instrument of expression, the body is a distinctive medium. Its movements can convey joy, fear, hate, anguish, every nuance of emotion. Travelers are often delighted to find how intelligible the motion of a hand or facial expression can be in place of a common language. After all, you don't need a dictionary to understand a woman's weeping. So it is that a Frenchman can understand a San Francisco policeman's message as he directs a busy intersection at rush hour. The job is simply to keep the traffic flowing, but every part of the traffic policeman's body is involved —the flourish of his arms, the fingers of his hands spread wide as he signals to the cars to stop, his arm curving and straightening, curving and straightening, his body turning in a semi-circle as the light changes. His legs bend, his body dips, his head tosses to urge on straggling pedestrians. The recurrent toot of the whistle hanging on his lower lip is set to a rhythmic pattern determined by the setting of red and green lights. Green light this way, red light that way—turn, raise, dodge and toot.

In the same way, Nigerian girls create a beautiful series of movements with the simple, everyday task of pounding the millet. Working the pestle in a down-and-up motion, they move in a lovely counter rhythm: they toss the pestle in the air, catch it, move the pestle down and up, toss it, catch the pestle, press down and toss again.

As the human body can bring rhythm and movement to everyday tasks, so it can recreate situations by exaggerating and abstracting these very movements in a mime. Think of the movement you would make to frighten somebody. Quite naturally, your body would lean forward, menacingly, the hand clenched in a fist raised in the air. You can see how stamping, shouting and waving is the most natural thing in the world. This principle is at work in the *Dea* dance of the Frafra people in northern Ghana. This dance is performed as a make-believe battle between the highland and lowland dwellers, and may well have originated from a hunter's stamping, shouting and swinging a club to frighten a wild animal. A soloist chants a taunting song while the other men reply with grunts to a rhythmic pattern of a hard stamp with the right foot, followed by a weak step with the left. On the other side of the world, the Japanese utilize this same psychology in karate: The fierce shout of a participant has a paralyzing effect on his opponent and in turn tends to support the shouter's own courage.

Recreating experience and exaggerating it in mime are natural to everyone. Every time a fisherman in any part of the world describes "the one that got away" the size of the fish increases. The distance between the narrator's hands grows larger every time the tale is told. In the same way, the African might spin out the story of a successful hunt with his body—his entire being is employed for the narrative. As the story is retold, the movements become smoother and smoother and smoother, and gradually they become part of an orderly sequence of movements. A dance is born!

Many African dances are mime versions of actual experiences. Harvest dances express thankfulness for the fruits of the earth. The movements of the *Sokodae*, a Ghanaian funeral dance, mimic the courtship of birds; while the women patiently step, step, step along, the men parade like gorgeous peacocks, bowing and strutting, with their brilliant clothes streaming behind them like bright tail feathers. The welcome of a child into the adult community in the puberty dance, or the farewell to the chief in the royal funeral dance—whatever the occasion, the particular dance that is used for it is an appropriate one. It is suited in both mood and style to the event and to the people who dance it.

The close association of dance movement with experience makes dances from tribe to tribe distinctive. For example, the *Dea* dance of the Frafra people of Ghana is extremely simple. In column formation, each dancer holds a sword in one hand and stamps down hard on his right foot, softly on his left. The feet and right hand alone are involved. In complete contrast are any of the half-dozen versions of the *Adowa* dance, which is danced by the Ashanti of Ghana. In this dance, the dancer's spins and turns involve the total body, the head, shoulders, arms, torsos and legs, the pattern determined by a musician striking a drum.

Differences in basic movements reflect the particular cultures that spawn the dances. Each society uses the body in specific ways. As each culture has its distinctive vocabulary, so in the dances different parts of the body—eyes, hands, feet, neck, shoulders, belly, ribs, toes—may be emphasized in distinctive movements.

Among the Akan people of Ghana, for instance, the Fante style is noted for rapid footwork while the Ashanti place emphasis on hand and arm movements. The Dagbani people make much of the ripples of the upper torso; intricate footwork distinguishes the *Akom* dance of the Akan; the Kiziba people focus attention on the larynx, the Kalahari bushmen give an inimitable picture of the antelope buck making comical leaps before the female. A subtle use of hip movement is distinguished by the Kalabari dancers of eastern Nigeria, while in western Nigeria, the Ijaw dancers display exciting variation in their foot movements.

In many dances, the movements are determined by the costumes. The whirling turns of the *Taki* dance make wide billowing shapes of the dancers full-flowing smocks. A chief's dance movements reflect his exalted status—they are well-controlled, partially because of the heavy jewelry he wears and the richly ornamented cloth draping his body which inhibits him from moving at any but a regally restrained pace.

When the rippling muscles of the stomach are a feature of the dance, a belt of cowrie shells may be worn. Extensions of hand movements are achieved with a whisk made from an oxtail or horsetail. Buzzers on the ankles of the Frafra dancers increase the interest of their simple stamping movement. When the South African Angoni perform the *Rain* dance, they break branches from trees and carry them as symbols of the growth that rain makes possible.

One of the most spectacular extensions of the human body is the ten-foot stilts of the Gagalo stilt dancers of Iwoye, West Yoruba in Nigeria. At the annual harvest festival in honor of their supernatural protector, Orisa, the stilt dance must be performed before the farmers may harvest their crop of yams. To achieve the phenomenal control of these mammoth stilts, the dancers are trained from childhood, beginning on miniature stilts and moving on to increasingly taller ones.

Similarly, the Ishan acrobats need years of daily practice before they acquire the perfect dexterity required for their performance in the *Ikhien-ani-mhin* dance.

Costumes and props, such as sticks, ladles and dumbbells, are used to dramatize a movement. But over all is the clear and committed dedication of the dancer to the performance. While the dance lasts, dancer and musician become so completely absorbed that a dance may continue for hours or days without loss of the performer's vitality or audience's interest. Because the audience expects the dance to reflect the community's traditional way of life, the reiteration of familiar forms is eagerly welcomed. It is a reassuring confirmation of the pattern of their daily lives. When there *is* a change in the dance, it is a reflection of new developments in the life-style of the community, not a consciously planned novelty.

The female mask for the Bedu moon ritual of Ghana is brightly colored with red and white clay and dwarfs the dancer who wears it.

Raffia disguises the male mask in the Bedu moon ritual of Ghana.

Costume and ornament play an important part in this dance of the Hausa people, performed by the Ghana dance ensemble.

The combination of killing heat, heavy weight of the masks and difficulty of the dance make this beautiful Dogon ritual supremely difficult to perform.

A spontaneous performance in a small west African village shows the important role of costume in the execution of a dance.

Ghanaian dancers mimic planting movements in a harvest ritual. Communal well-being is emphasized in the final phase of the Bawa harvest dance.

THE MASKS OF TRADITIONAL AFRICAN DANCE

You see but the shine on a goat's eyebrow. [*You only see the surface, the real meaning is hidden.*]

African saying

The masks and headdresses used in traditional African dances reflect their spirit and meaning. To "dance the mask" reveals and defines thoughts and feelings about life which the community shares and has always shared. Large, beautiful and brightly colored, the masks are important symbols in the traditional dances of many African tribes.

When a mask covers a dancer's face, the dancer can escape the restriction of his body. He is no longer recognized as himself, because the stylized mask transforms him into the spirit of the mask, a link between man and the gods and ancestors, who control his life. The spirit of the dance emerges from the dancer's mouth.

Usually carved of wood the masks are woefully vulnerable to the natural enemies of wood—termites and time. Because of this, almost all masks in use today are less than a hundred years old. They reflect an unchanging tradition despite their relative "newness": Just as most dance is created for a specific occasion, the masks are carved to order for a specific ritual, their shape and ornamentation determined by the nature of the dance, its function and its symbolism.

The men who carve these masks are as valued as the dancers who perform in them. A carver of superior skill will often be commissioned to prepare masks for nearby villages which do not boast a master carver of their own community. The close tie between mask and dance is epitomized in the Dogon practice of requiring each man to be his own carver.

One of the most beautiful masks is made for the *Tyi Wara* ritual of the Bambara people of Mali. The Tyi Wara Koun, as the headdress is known, is distinguished by its abstract flowing lines, in the shape of man and animal. The long horns are said to represent hearing, the sense through which man's courage is aroused. The tapered face supposedly represents the anteater, the symbol of strength and endurance.

Traditionally, the Tyi Wara Koun is made of the hard wood of the Toro tree which is fairly resistant to wood beetles and termites. It is sometimes decorated with small scraps of red cloth, and metalwork. After it is rubbed to a deep maroon color, it is set on a wooden base from which a veil of raffia hangs. The raffia is first dyed a deep black, then braided and sewn into a veil about four feet long, which completely camouflages the dancer's face. The dancer wears a woven cotton or burlap shirt decorated with strings of fiber sewn on it.

Raffia is also worn with masks in the dance of the *Bedu* moon, a December festival of the Nafana people of Ghana. These huge masks are carved whole from the Onyina tree masked, the female figure stands over ten feet tall and the male figure stands between seven and nine feet. The *Bedu* festival is a purification rite in which the dancers visit every house in the village to bless it. The masks absorb all the evil and misfortune of the old year, and by the time the festival is over, the village is cleansed for a new beginning as the new year approaches.

The cultures of traditional African society are full of examples of similar rituals against the power of evil spirits, sickness and misfortune. The Gelede masqueraders of Nigeria perform a masked dance to persuade witches not to use their supernatural powers for evil purposes. The marvelous female masks with pointed wooden breasts used in this dance represent the good things in life, which can resist the fiendish practices of the witches.

The masked dance of the Bété people of the Ivory Coast is a fine example of the close tie between the use of the mask and the refusal of a people to be bested by a hostile environment. Settled in an area of stubborn soil and unfriendly climate, to dance the mask for The Bété is essential to their resistance to disease and to their persistence in forcing crops to grow. Trainees of the masked dance must study and practice their roles for years mastering drum dance and song. So highly developed is The Bété masking tradition one village has trained sacrificial white chickens to perch quietly on top of the mask throughout a violent dance.

One of the most spectacular masked dances is the *Ekpo* ritual of the Bini people of Nigeria. The purpose of this ritual is to keep the town clean, in a state of ritual purity, and to emphasize the good health of the people. The rite lasts several days, during which time the dancers visit every house where they are rewarded with coins and kola nuts in exchange for their prayers. The dancers represent Obo and Agboghidi, the heroic figure who founded the Ekpo cult. Both of these dancers wear black masks to symbolize their ability to heal.

The white man in the *Ekpo* ritual, called Ebo (the Bini word for white man), reflects the African sense of humor. Though Africans had been trading with Europe for many centuries, most Africans had never really seen a white man until the colonial era in the eighteenth and nineteenth centuries. Traditionally, white skin is a sign of illness in Africa, and evil spirits often wear white masks. Ebo represents the British district officer, the efficient administrator; he is an incongruous amusement in this ritual dedicated to health, fertility and communal purification.

The Dogon people of Mali are famous for their striking geometric masks, sometimes as high as twelve feet, made of geometric crosses. These crosses have several interpretations as symbols of divine order and equilibrium. They may also represent a bird in flight, and some people believe that the masks represent the crocodile who carried the Dogon across the Niger River to their homeland. This masked dance is performed on many occasions, including funerals of honored men. At one of the funeral dances the widow carries the calabash she was given on the day of her engagement. Two weeks after the burial, her dead husband is honored with a masked dance.

Masked dances are performed on many important occasions, from purification rituals to hunting dances to funerals. It is a major event, and the dancers prepare for it from early childhood. It is not enough that a dancer can move around under a heavy mask in killing heat; the masked dance must be danced supremely well. The masks link the dancer to the forces which shape the world.

The small face surmounting this mask is an exaggerated form of the larger face, with typical Bambara features.

Another bush cow mask, this one made by the Grunsi people of Upper Volta, features elaborate surface decoration and has a very human quality.

Variations in the *Tyi Wara* ("working animal")
masks include female, left, with small antelope
behind and male, right and center.

A female mask of the Bobo people with stylized nose, eyes and markings. Note the grip at the bottom which helps the dancer hold and balance the mask.

This Mossi mask from Upper Volta combines a stylized face divided by a row of small pyramids with the simple horns of an antelope, all painted in bright geometric patterns. The human figure above is unpainted.

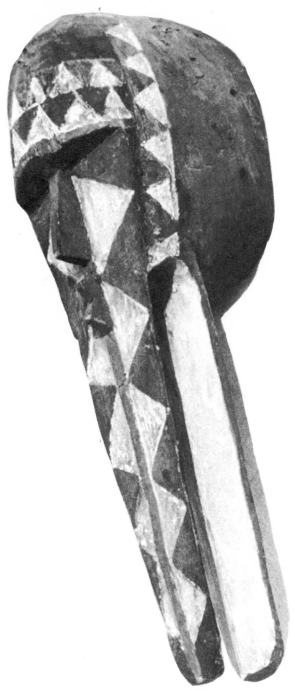

Horizontally, this Yatenga mask looks like a crocodile or a bird. Head-on, it looks like a human
face, with the jaw/beak suggesting a beard or a
body under it.

This bush cow mask is made from a single piece
of heavy wood. Notice the crouching human
figure in the forehead of this stylized mask.

The female figure has her arms raised in an appeal
for rain in the Bambara style.

THE MIGRATION OF TRADITIONAL AFRICAN DANCE

The foot has no nose.

African saying

The African heritage is like a flowing river. As it carries along its past in its forward movement, as it is fed by waters of the streams that flow into it, its essential identity never changes. Thousands of miles from its origin and altered by alien customs and traditions, the heritage of African dance has never been destroyed, even by the oppression and degradation of slavery. The history of the dance in the New World has been strongly influenced by the African slaves who were shipped to the Americas.

By the fifteenth century, Europeans had begun to colonize Africa, and to send her wealth, including silk, kola nuts, perfume, sugar and rice. With the increasing demand for sugar in Europe, huge sugar plantations were developed in the West Indies. The need for cheap labor on these plantations made West Africa's most valuable resource her people. Millions of West Africans were captured and taken to the West Indies as slave labor for sugar production. The slave trade began to dominate European activity in West Africa in 1600, when about a million slaves were transported, a number that spiralled over the years to an awesome seven million by the eighteenth century.

In Haiti, in Savannah, Georgia, everywhere black slaves lived in the New World, dance began to reflect African influences. Dances such as the *Turkey trot*, the *Eagle rock* and *Ballin' the jack* are all branches on the same tree, a tree that has its roots in Africa. Sometimes the interrelationship of the dances in Africa and the Western World becomes so entwined, it resembles the back-and-forth debate on which came first, the chicken or the egg. However, there are patterns that emerge, and at least two distinct trends can be traced.

On the other hand, there are dances that retain their meanings and traditions, and remain true relatives of their African forerunners. The ritual dances of traditional Africa still survive in the Americas as Voodoo. In Haiti, the *Voodoo* rite of Dahomey remains, with few changes, as the slaves brought it centuries ago. Its dependence on a drum accompaniment identifies it with Africa, and the traditional requirements of certain kinds of drums—a small boula drum, a middle-sized aguida and the large manman drum—clinches its African ties. Made of mahogany, oak, and cedar, these drums are specially dedicated and used solely for ritual purposes.

Only those who have been initiated into the Voodoo cult may participate in the rite. After a ceremony of greeting the priests, the dancers are taken possession of by a god, called Loa. The action is described as "being ridden" by a Loa while the priests leap and scream and whirl into a trance. The drums command the action of the *Voodoo* dance with special rhythmic patterns but the priest directs the drums with his rattle, a gourd filled with seeds which is called an asson. This series of movements is analogous to the *Possession* dance described earlier in which the priest twirls and spins faster and faster in an effort to propel himself out of a trance.

While the Haitian *Voodoo* rite comes from Dahomey, Cuban Blacks derive their *Voodoo* tradition from Yorubaland in Nigeria. The traditional symbolism of the Yoruba *Voodoo* dance is retained in the *Santeria*. What appears to be disorganized chaos to an outsider is in fact ecstasy of movement, which is totally related to the meaning of the dance.

On the other hand, we can see in the migration and development of the *Calenda* (a fertility and courting dance from the coast of Guinea), how African dances change as they are removed from the traditions and people who fostered them. The *Calenda* is the grandfather of the French *Sarabande*, a popular dance among the nobility of the eighteenth century. The *Sarabande* is a formal dance which came to Spain from the Arab conquerers, and in turn from Spain to France. Altered greatly in its travels and adopted by people who had no idea of its origins or meanings, the *Sarabande* has no real connection with the *Calenda*, even though its origin in the *Calenda* is established.

In the same way, many popular dances developed from the *Calenda* as the slaves taught their traditional dance to the Spanish. The Cuban *Yuka*, which is derived from the *Calenda* through the *Yuka* dance of Chad in Central Africa, is more stylized than its parent, but it still has significance for the participants in fertility and courtship.

From the *Yuka* developed the American *Rumba*, which was introduced at the World's Fair in 1932 in Chicago. A popular ballroom dance, it retains far less of the meaning and symbolism of the *Calenda* than the Yuka.

The *Fandango*, the national dance of Spain, is also derived from the *Calenda*. In Haiti, the *Fandango* is known as *Loaloachi*, a religious dance. Again, the basic movements of the *Calenda* survive, as the dancer strives to move the hips and the lower part of the body, while the rest of the body remains practically motionless.

The *Rumba*, the *Fandango* and the American *Shimmy* are all sisters under the skin. Their common mother is the *Calenda*, the African fertility dance. The *Black Bottom*, the *Charleston* and the *Foxtrot* of our "Roaring Twenties" are also echoes of the same African original. Yet stripped of their specific meanings, they can no longer be considered African. Many basic conventions of African traditional dance have disappeared—for example, dancing in couples is very unusual in African dance. Just as it is awkward to dance in Western fashion to African rhythms, it is equally impossible to remove the meaning and function of a dance without changing it as an expression of African culture. When the young Sara girls and boys of Chad in Central Africa danced to the rhythms of the Yuka drum in a version of the *Calenda*, with the drummer wearing a pair of maracas on his wrists to protect his drum from evil spirits, it was an authentic dance of courtship. Metamorphosed into the *Rumba*, it is an erotic and graceful dance with lovely movements, but its African origin is a dim memory, far away in time and place on the African continent.

The Ghana Dance Ensemble practices the basic movements of the Atsiabegkor dance, which combines stylizations of western arms drill with traditional war movements.

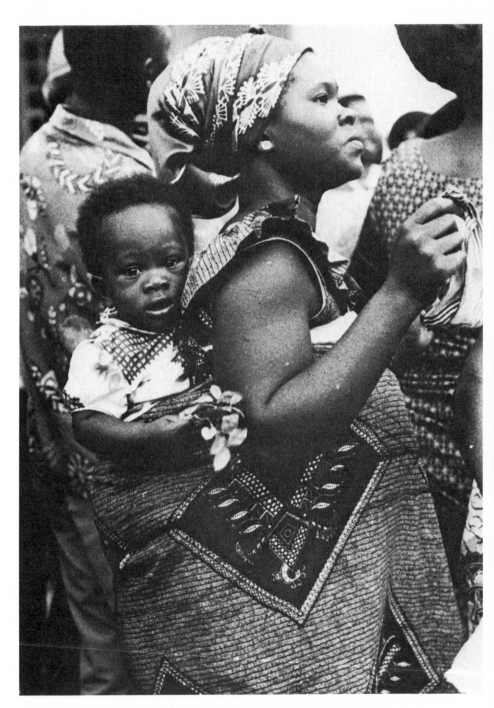

A woman dances in the loosely structured Akpasa groups, in which everyone participates in casual dances, according to the feeling he gets from the music.

A priestess in training dances into a trance during a healing ceremony in western Africa.

Two Ghanaian girls dancing the Kpanlago, a recreational dance in the Highlife tradition.

The drummers are a crucial part of any dance troupe. Here they accompany a priest in an animal dance of West Africa.

Crowds gather to watch a rehearsal of the Bawa harvest celebration of Ghana.

AFRICA IN TRANSITION

*The shortest and fastest road to the future
is through the past.*

Aimé Césaire

On March 6, 1957, the British colony called Gold Coast
proclaimed itself the independent country of Ghana. It
was the first black independent state of modern Africa.
In less than a decade, thirty more African countries followed Ghana's lead to the state of independence and to
a new consciousness of African identity.

Centuries of mingling with foreigners, from the traders
of Portugal to the civil servants of the British Empire,
have left their mark on all aspects of African life—education, religion, transportation, and commerce. Dressed in
Western-style clothing, the Kenyan walking down Tom
Mboya Street in Nairobi is indistinguishable from a stroller
along Union Street in San Francisco. Yet the Kenyan's
essense is African, nourished by a cultural heritage which
has stubbornly preserved its soul during all the long and
brutal years of foreign assault.

Africa is in a state of change, and the traditional performing arts which have always been a vital means of expression in daily life have been influenced by Western ideas. Yet the arts remain African in that they continue to define the African way of life, even though attitudes and behavior are somewhat more modern. Neither life in Africa nor its dance forms have remained static. The African's responsiveness to a changing world is seen everywhere except in the most remote areas. Yet in the old African way, as the life-style changes, so does the dance.

As long as a village remains untouched by the influences of modern society, its traditional way of life persists. And in that way of life, the dances formed for and by it continue without significant change. But once Africa was roused to break away from the oppression of colonialism, it emerged rapidly into the modern world of industrial growth and technological development. With technology comes records, radio and television to make the Africans, particularly the young, impatient to join the world "outside." Technology improves transportation as well, bringing tourists representing many alternative life-styles to Africa. The effects are evident in many African cities, which increasingly resemble those of the West.

As more and more African countries achieved independence, they needed to rediscover their rich artistic heritages from which they had been alienated by colonialism. They needed to reassert their African identity in a contemporary idiom, and to present this legacy to Africans and non-Africans alike.

Governments played a key role in the cultural revival in Africa. In 1963, Sierra Leone sent a national dance troupe to the New York World's Fair which represented various cultural traditions of the country. Forty-five dancers, singers, and musicians, ranging in age from seven to sixty, were chosen to perform authentic traditional dances. They were enthusiastically received, and still perform for tourists and at official government functions.

African pride was evident in 1969 when thirty-eight African countries sent about six thousand representatives to Algiers for the First Pan African Cultural Festival. On the same July day the American astronauts took their first step on the moon, the headline spread across the front page of the official government newspaper: AFRICANS TO ALGIERS TO CELEBRATE THEIR LIBERATION AND THEIR UNITY. The first landing on the moon was relegated to page 6.

There are many such examples of using the past as the road to the future. Art festivals and national dance troupes are deeply involved in the dual task of preserving traditional forms and presenting them in new settings. Heart Beat, a government-sponsored group of dancers from Uganda, was formed in 1963 as a result of a nationwide competition, which was held in conjunction with Uganda's independence celebration. The troupe has traveled all over the world presenting their dancers to a variety of spectators. The national troupe of Mali has incorporated its diverse cultural heritage into a single repertoire of traditional dances, modifying them for theater audiences all over the world.

Certain changes from the originals are obvious. Where once firelight provided illumination, now theater lamps give light. Performances are limited to three hours to accommodate western theater conventions. The stage can only hold a given number of performers, regardless of how many participants the traditional form of the dance demands. Approval is expressed by polite applause at set intervals, Western style, rather than the traditional joining in, or running up to a dancer to place a coin on his forehead, to be glued there by the dancer's sweat.

The purification rite of the Bini people now takes place not only in the villages, but on Nigerian television. Another Nigerian group, the Mbari Mbayo Club, held a three day seminar on dancing and drumming for academics and artists from the West, both testaments to the widening interest and the increasing sophistication in African arts. The strong international interest in black arts resulted in the International Festival of Negro Arts in Dakar, held in April, 1966. The contributions of blacks to cultures everywhere—Brazil, Haiti, Jamaica and the United States—were reflected in the performances at the festival. As Léopold Sédar Senghor said in the opening address of the Festival:

> *Slavery belongs in the past—Negro art sustains us in our determination to live by our poets, short story writers, and novelists, our singers and dancers, our painters and sculptors, our musicians; whether they paint violent mystical abstractions or the noble elegance of royal African courtships, whether they dance the Development Plan or sing of the diversification of the crops, the Negro African artists help us to live more intensely, to live better, to resolve the problem of our future.*

The aim of this, and other African art festivals, is to encourage dance troupes to move away from their communities in order to display their people's culture and to exchange materials and learn each other's art forms. Obviously, this must have an effect on the dances so shared. Performed over television, at festivals and in theaters, dances have lost their bond with the way of life that gave them birth.

When the people of the same ethnic group move away from home to work or live in another place, they often join dance societies to practice and perform dances of their home area. It is not an unfamiliar part of the American scene: Los Angeles has its Iowa Club, New York, its Sons of Eire; San Francisco, The Rose and Thistle Club for homesick Englishmen. Whenever people find themselves in an alien land or way of life, they seek out the companionship of those who share their heritage.

What is happening to African dance is the continuing process of change. An example is the treatment of Christian themes with a particular African touch: in Cameroon, a local priest and musicologist Abbé Ngumu has Africanized the Catholic mass, replacing the Gregorian chant with tribal rhythms, gestures and dances, and translating the words into a local language, Ewondo. "Young mothers clutching babies dance in a trance to the altar to receive the Host," says Abbé Ngumu. "These dances are pagan in origin, less devotional than a mass in Europe, but it suits the African soul."

Dance is communication between oneself and one's people and between oneself and the universe. It is a rich and vital ancient expression and remains a primary art

55

enduringly in African cultures. No number of foreign films, music, literature, paintings or dances will ever eliminate this primary expression of the African.

That musty old cliché, "Every African can dance" is based on a reality, for basic to the African way of life is the response of the body to express an emotion and the unity of the body and soul. The superb African cultures survived colonial conquest and now as Africa rediscovers her heritage, Westerners are discovering Africa's beauty.

The Bambaya dance of the Dagbani people of West Africa is
marked by dignity and grace.

The Ghana Dance Ensemble practices character-istic movements of many dances from different areas of the country.

AFRICAN DANCES:
INSTRUCTIONS

I am a Negro
Black as the night is black
Black as the depths of my Africa

Langston Hughes

CHA CHA KOFI SA

This is a singing game played in a group with a leader. It originated among the Ga people of Ghana but is now played by many Ghanians. The leader sings and the group echos him, at the same time copying his movements.

This is a good warm-up exercise if you are interested in mastering some of the basic movements of African dance.

During this singing game, the dancer moves his body in a slow semi-circle, keeping his feet still. He stands with his feet slightly apart, and he can rock back and forth in time to the music.

♩ = ca. 108

Cha Cha Kuli   ChaCha Kofi Sa   Kofi Sa Lange

Cha Cha Hi Lunga   Cum a-dende

60

Begin with hands at the sides, knees slightly flexed, feet apart.

Raise hands to head.

Move hands to shoulders, with fingertips resting on shoulders.

Move hands to hips, arms bent, with fingertips touching hips.

Move hands to knees, touching kneecaps with fingertips. The song is repeated, and the dancer moves up the body in reverse sequence.

PASSING GAME

In order to get acquainted with the rhythms of African music, you might want to play this game that is popular with Ghanaian teenagers. Since by African standard any movement to music constitutes a dance, this is considered dance play.

Sit in a circle, either on the ground, or in chairs around a table. Each participant has a stone or a potato, or any object that is easy to handle and fairly compact.

On the first beat, the object is set down to the right.

On the second beat, the object is picked up.

On the third beat it is shifted to the right hand from the left hand, and

passed to the right on the fourth beat.

When a participant misses a beat, he is eliminated from the game. Much excitement ensues when only two participants are left. This game requires a surprising amount of concentration and coordination.

While the game is going on, this song, which is Ga in origin, is sung by the participants, echoing a leader.

i- wa de de dee Sen- i-wa o-se me ye den Sen- i-wa de de dee Sen-

i-wa o-se be di di Sen- i-wa de de dee Sen- i-wa Eben(a)du-ba nia

Sen

-i-wa de de dee Sen- i-wa Fu-fu n'a-ban-kwan   de de dee Sen-

Sen-i-wa

*

i-wa Ko si naa de Sen- i-wa de de dee Sen- i-wa Mmo-fra   Sen-

nkye nio

*spoken

67

i-wa de de dee Sen- i-wa Npanyinminson Sen i-wa de de dee Sen-

i-wa Sen-i-wa de de dee Sen- i-wa

THE HIGHLIFE

When Ghana became an independent country, President Kwame Nkhrumah instituted many cultural programs, including several in the dance. He made the *Adowa*, which originated as a dignified funeral dance among the Ashanti people of Ghana, the national dance. The *Adowa*, with its graceful movements became popular among the Fante and Ga peoples of Ghana as well.

With increased Western influence in music and dance, the Highlife emerged. Using the basic steps of the Adowa, this version of the highlife utilizes improvisation and a lively beat to give a more modern and more Western feel. Here is the highlife, as it is danced among the citizens of Accra, the capital city of Ghana. In this version, couples face each other (in the style of the *Boogaloo*), but do not touch, or else dance face to face, embracing in the style of the waltz.

The posture of the dancers gives this dance its characteristic look. The torso should be thrown forward slightly (about 20°) and the neck and head should be held loosely, moving as the music inclines the dancer to move.

The arms are held close to the body, bent at the elbow so that the forearms are held stiffly forward a little below the waist. The hands should be relaxed and move with a slight circular motion with the music. The feet should be together at the start of each new step. The knees should be held as stiffly as possible. The steps are repeated six or eight times in succession, but this is up to the whims of you and your partner.

1. Step forward with the right foot. Slightly lift left heel, keeping the left toe on the ground. Bring the right foot back beside the left foot. The right foot swings

Step forward with the left foot. Slightly lift the right heel with the toes remaining on the ground. Bring the left foot back beside the right foot, keeping the right heel raised. The left foot swings forward about 4″ and lands on the ground.

2. Step forward and to the left with the left foot. Bring the right foot next to the left foot.

Step forward and to the right with the right foot. Bring the left foot next to the right foot. Halt.

3. Step forward and to the right with the right foot. Bring the left foot next to the right foot. With the left foot cross over the right foot. Shift weight to the left foot. Bring the right foot to the right of left foot.

Step forward and to the left with the left foot. Bring the right foot next to the left foot. Shift weight to the right foot. Bring the left foot to the left of the right foot.

SANDE ZIZEI DANCE
of the Loma Tribe of Lofa County, Liberia
This dance is performed by Liberian teenagers in bush school. It is always danced in a group, either in a circle or in several lines. This dance is a simplified group version of Kpazegi dances which are taught as a part of the Sande initiation. This a traditional dance which is uninfluenced by Western styles.

1. The left foot steps forward about 3″ ahead of the right foot with a slight stamping to emphasize the beat.

Then the left foot is brought back to a position 3″ behind the right foot with the same stamping to emphasize the beat.

As the left foot leads, the right arm is held across the chest, the elbow lifted and held slightly forward. The left arm with the hand extended points down and away from the body at a 45° angle.

The dancer watches a spot on the ground about the spot where the extended left arm and hand are pointing.

The same sequence is repeated with the right foot. The right foot is brought forward 3″ ahead of the left with slight stamping for emphasis.

The right foot is brought back to a position 3″ behind the right foot with the same stamping to emphasize the beat.

When the right foot leads, the left arm is held slightly raised and across the chest. The right hand extended and the right arm pointing out and away from the body at a 45° angle.

The dancer watches a spot on the ground about where the extended right arm and hand are pointed.

This sequence is repeated eight times. The dancers turn around during the third and fourth and again during the sixth and seventh sequences.

2. This step is like running in place.

The right foot slides rapidly back until the right toe is even with the left heel and the right heel is raised. The weight falls on the left foot.

Glance over the right shoulder when the right foot and arm go back.

The forearms point forward, the elbows held at the sides, the wrists limp and the hands dangling. The right arm and hand are thrown down and back in a fanning action at the same time that the right foot slides back.

Then the left foot slides back until the left toes are even with the right heel and the left heel is raised.

The left arm and hand make the same downward and backward fanning motion while the left foot is sliding back.

Glance over the left shoulder when the left foot and arm go back.

This sequence is repeated five times.

3. The right foot steps out 4" to the side, the left step 3" forward, then the right foot slides over so that

the ball of the foot and toe touch the instep of the left foot (but the weight of the body remains on the left foot) and the right foot steps out again.

This step is repeated three times and the dancer moves to the right.

The left foot steps out 4″ to the left side, the right foot steps three inches forward, then the left foot slides over so that the ball of the foot and the toe touch the instep of the right foot (but the weight of the body remains on the right foot) and the left foot steps out to the side again.

This step is repeated three times moving the dancer to the left.

Forearms are held forward, elbows not less than 120° angle, wrists limp and hands dangling. The arms and hips swing to the right or to the left along with the body movement. The gaze is straight ahead, looking neither left or right.

This sequence is repeated twice.

4. This step involves swivel-walking on heel and toe of one foot.

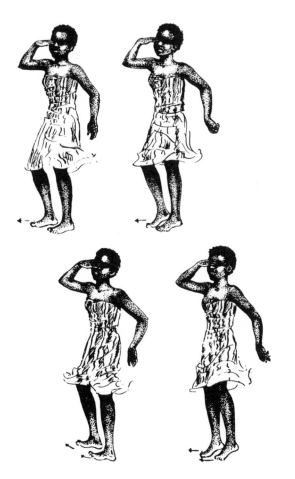

The right foot is raised completely by flexing the knee. The left foot pivots first on the heel and then on the toe shuffling the dancer four swivel steps to the right. The ball and toe of the right foot are allowed to skim the ground to keep balance.

The right arm is raised, the right hand cocked forward at eye level when the dancer moves to the right on the left foot. The left hand and arm are down and away from the body to balance.

The left foot is raised completely by flexing the knee. The right foot pivots first on the heel and then on the toe shuffling the dancer four swivel steps to the left. The ball and toe of the left foot are allowed to skim the ground to keep balance.

The left arm is raised, the left hand cocked forward at eye level while the dancer moves to the left on the right foot. The right hand and arm are held down and away from the body to balance.

The gaze is directed toward the audience.

This sequence is repeated 8 times.

BIBLIOGRAPHY
AND
DISCOGRAPHY

Books

AMMAH, Charles, *Ga Homowo*, Accra, Ghana: Advance Publishing Company, 1968

BANFIELD, Beryle, *Africa in the Curriculum*, New York: Edward W. Blyden Press, Inc., 1968

BOHANNON, Paul, *Africa and Africans*, Garden City, New York: Doubleday and Co., 1948

DAVIDSON, Basil, *The African Genius*, Boston: Little, Brown and Co., 1969

FAGE, J. D., *Atlas of African History*, New York: St. Martin's Press, 1958

FAGG, William and Plass, Margaret, *African Sculpture*, New York: E. P. Dutton, 1964

GORER, Geofrrey, *Africa Dances*, WW Norton and Co., Inc., New York: 1962

GRIAULE, M. Marcel, *Folk Art of Black Africa*, New York: Tudor Publishing Co., 1950

HERSHKOVITZ, Melville, *The Human Factor in Changing Africa*, New York: Random House Inc., 1958

HUGHES, Langston, *The First Book of Africa*, New York: Franklin Watts, Inc., 1965

JANHEINZ, Jahn, *Muntu, The New African Culture*, New York: Grove Press, 1961

LYSTAD, Robert, *The African World*, New York: Frederick A. Praeger, 1965

MERRIAM, Alan, *A Prologue to the Study of African Arts*, Yellow Springs: Antoich Press, 1962

NKETIA, H. J. Kwabena, *Music, Dance and Drama*, Legon, Ghana: University of Ghana, 1965

OPOKU, A. M. *African Dances: A Ghanaian Profile*, Legon: University of Ghana, 1965

ROBERTS, John Storm. *Black Music of Two Worlds*, New York: Praeger Publishers, 1972
SUTHERLAND, Efua. *Playtime in Africa*, New York: Atheneum, 1968
TUFUO, J. W. and C. E. Donkor. *Ashantis of Ghana*. Accra: Anowuo Educational Publications, 1969

Magazines

Africa Report, 500 Dupont Circle, Washington D.C. 20036
African Arts, African Studies Center, University of California, Los Angeles, California 90024
African Forum Quarterly, 720 Fifth Avenue, New York 10019
Africana Library Journal, African Publishing Corporation, 1010 Fifth Avenue, New York 10003
Research Review, Institute of African Studies, University of Ghana, Legon, Ghana
The New African, 12-A Goodwins Court, London, W.C. 2, England

Records

Africa: East and West (Institute of Ethnomusicology, University of California, Los Angeles)
African Music from the French Colonies (Columbia)

African Rhythms, The Exciting Sounds of Guy Warren
  (Decca)
Anthology of African Music, UNESCO Collection
  Barenreiter-Musicaphon)
The Baule of the Ivory Coast (Folkways)
Ewe Music of Ghana (Folkways)
Music of the Cameroons (Folkways)
Music of The Diola-Fogny of the Casamance, Senegal
  (Folkways)
The Music of the Jos Plateau and Other Regions of Nigeria
  (Folkways)
New Sounds From A New Nation—Ghana (Tempo)
New Sounds From A New Nation—Guinea (Tempo)
The Topoke People of the Congo (Folkways)

Other Resource Material
African Arts Study Kits, a series of curricular materials, including illustrated booklets and film strips, available from

African Studies Center
University of California
Los Angeles, California 90024

Tape recorder cassettes, dance and drum music, available from

Institute of African Studies
University of Ghana
Legon, Ghana

INDEX

Kalahari Tribesmen, 26
Karate, 25
Kenya, 51
Kingship, 12
Konifemo, 11
Konte, 8
Krapzegi Dances, 74
Krachi People, 7
Kundum Festival, 10
Kuper, Hilda, 2
Lion, 12
Lipschitz, Jacques, 5
Loa, 44
Loaloachi, 46
Lobi People, 20
Loma Tribe, 74
Los Angeles, 55
Mali, 8, 34, 36, 53
Mask Spirit, 33
Maari Mboyo Club, 54
Mime, 24f
Mohammed, 20
Mousso Koroni, 9
Mountain, 12
Millet, 24
Nafama People, 34
Nairobi, 51
New York, 55
New York World's Fair, 53
N'gala Tyi, 9
Ngumu, Abbe, 55
Nigeria, 4, 20, 24, 25, 45, 54
Nigerians, 9
Nkrumah, Kwame, 68
Nmaaduum, 11
Nmaa Faa, 11
Ntwaaho, 21
Obo, 36
Ofufuri, 7
Onyina tree, 34
Orisa, 27
Pan-African Cultural
    Conference, 53
Passover, 10
Physical Exercise, 23

Policeman, 24
Possession Dance, 4, 45
Priest, 21, 44
Purification, 4
Raffia, 34
Religion, 12
Ritual, 6ff, 12
Rose and Thistle Club, 55
Rumba, 46
Savannah, 44
Sarabande, 45
Sande Initiation, 74
Sande Zizei Dance, 74ff.
San Francisco, 51, 55
Santeria Dance, 44
Senghor, Léopold Sédar, 54
Sex Roles, 21
Sierra Leone, 52
Singing, 3, 7
Slavery, 43f
Sokodae Dance, 25
South Africa, 37
Sons of Eire, 55
Spain, 45
Swazi People, 2ff
Swaziland, 12
Technology, 52
Theatre, 53
Uganda, 53
Voodoo, 44
Tyi-n-gana, 9
Tyi Wara, 9
Tyi Wara Dance, 8f
Tyi Wara Koun, 34f
West Indies, 43
Wizard, 3
Women, Role of, 12